Contents

How to use this book

Each page has a title telling you what it is about.

Instructions look like this. Always read these carefully before starting.

This shows you how to set out your work. The first question is done for you.

Ask your teacher if you need to do these.

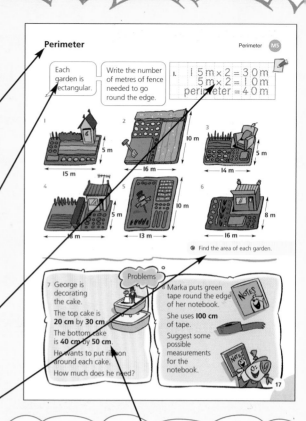

Read these word problems carefully. Decide how you will work out the answers.

Sometimes there is a **Hint** to help you.

Sometimes you need materials to help you.

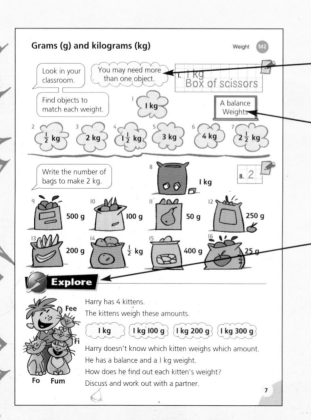

This shows that the activity is an **Explore**. Work with a friend.

This means you must decide how to set out your work and show your workings.

Centimetres (cm)

Measure the length of each pencil in cm.

1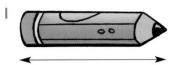

1. 4 cm

2

3

4

5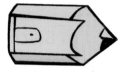

6

7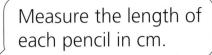

e Write each length in mm.

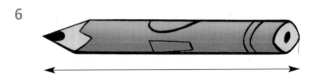

Find each object.

Estimate, then measure each length in cm and mm.

8. estimate 16 cm
length 17 cm 3mm

8

9

10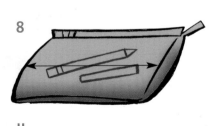

11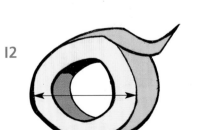

12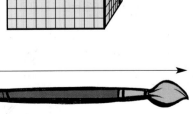

13

Write the number of cm.

1   **1 m 20 cm**

1. **120 cm**

2   **1 m 5 cm**

3   **20 mm**

4   **1 m 80 cm**

5   **2 m 30 cm**

6   **40 mm**

7   **1 m 56 cm**

Write the number of m and cm.

8   **130 cm**

8. **1 m 30 cm**

9   **220 cm**

10   **350 cm**

11   **200 cm**

Write the number of cm and mm.

12   **54 mm**

12. **5 cm 4 mm**

13   **68 mm**

14   **97 mm**

15   **60 mm**

4

Metres (m) and kilometres (km)

Write each distance walked in km and m.

1
I walked 2543 m.

1. 2 km 5 4 3 m

2
I walked 3342 m.

3
I walked 2230 m.

4
I walked 4100 m.

5
I walked 6012 m.

6
I walked 1111 m.

7
I walked 3921 m.

8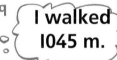
I walked 3403 m.

9
I walked 1045 m.

e Each walk took them to a shop and back. How far was each shop?

Write each distance from London in miles.

10. 300 ÷ 5 = 60
60 × 3 = 1 8 0 miles

5 km is about 3 miles.

	10 Manchester	11 Lincoln	12 John O'Groats	13 Edinburgh	14 Cardiff	15 Plymouth	16 Wimbledon	17 Lands End	18 Luton	19 Oxford	20 Brighton
London	300 km	100 km	1000 km	650 km	250 km	350 km	10 km	500 km	50 km	90 km	85 km

Grams (g) and kilograms (kg)

Write how many grams.

1 1 kg 700 g

1. 1 7 0 0 g

2 1 kg 200 g

3 2 kg 300 g

4 3 kg 150 g

5 1 kg 900 g

6 4 kg 100 g

7 $2\frac{1}{2}$ kg

Write how many kilograms and grams.

8 1500 g

8. 1 kg 500 g

9 2300 g

10 1700 g

11 3000 g

12 4500 g

13 1050 g

14 2505 g

15 1675 g

16 1225 g

Grams (g) and kilograms (kg)

Look in your classroom.

You may need more than one object.

1. 1 kg
Box of scissors

Find objects to match each weight.

| 1 kg

A balance
Weights

2 $\frac{1}{2}$ kg

3 2 kg

4 $1\frac{1}{2}$ kg

5 3 kg

6 4 kg

7 $2\frac{1}{2}$ kg

---

8 1 kg

Write the number of bags to make 2 kg.

8. 2

9 500 g

10 100 g

11  50 g

12  250 g

13 200 g

14 $\frac{1}{2}$ kg

15 400 g

16 25 g

Explore

Fee

Fi

Fo   Fum

Harry has 4 kittens.

The kittens weigh these amounts.

| 1 kg   1 kg 100 g   1 kg 200 g   1 kg 300 g

Harry doesn't know which kitten weighs which amount.

He has a balance and a 1 kg weight.

How does he find out each kitten's weight?

Discuss and work out with a partner.

Grams (g) and kilograms (kg)

Decide which unit (g or kg) you would use to weigh each object.

Estimate its weight.

1. grams
   estimate 400 g

1
2
3
4
5
6
7
8

Problems

9 Mr and Mrs Squirrel store **1 kg** of nuts for winter.

Together they eat **200 g** of nuts each month, starting in November.

How many grams of nuts are left on March 1st?

10 The vet is cross with Sam.

His dog Spot is overweight.

Spot weighs **25 kg**.

Sam puts Spot on a diet.

He loses **2½ kg**.

What is Spot's new weight?

Sam's gran looks after Spot for a week.

He puts on **¾ kg**.

What is Spot's weight now?

Millilitres (ml) and litres (l)

Write how many millilitres in each container.

1. 1 2 0 0 ml

Write how many litres and millilitres.

10. 1 l 7 0 0 ml

10 1700 ml

11  2300 ml

12  2500 ml

13  2650 ml

14  1850 ml

15  1900 ml

16  4000 ml

17  1500 ml

18  2350 ml

9

Litres and pints

Write how many pints of milk are in each churn.

I litre is about 2 pints.

1. **8 pints**

1. 4 l
2. 3 l
3. 2 l
4. $6\frac{1}{2}$ l
5. 7 l
6. 12 l
7. $8\frac{1}{2}$ l
8. $5\frac{1}{2}$ l
9. 15 l

Write how many litres of milk.

10. **I litre**

10. 2 pints

11. 7 pints

12. 4 pints

13. 3 pints

14. 9 pints

ℓ How much more, in litres, to fill each crate?

Litres (l) and millilitres (ml)

How much does it cost to fill each petrol tank?

1. Petrol 75p per litre

20 l tank

1. $20 \times 75p$
$= 1500p$
$= £15$

2. 40 l tank

3. 30 l tank

4. 50 l tank

5. 10 l tank

6. 100 l tank

7. 110 l tank

Problems

8 Simmi is ill.

She has **5 ml** of medicine after every meal, **3 times** a day.

She starts the medicine after tea on Monday evening.

She finishes the medicine after lunch on Friday.

How much medicine has she had?

9 Len buys **1 litre** of fizzy lemon.

He and 3 friends each drink the same amount.

There is **200 ml** of fizzy lemon left.

How much did they each drink?

11

Area

The squares are square centimetres.

Write the area of each rectangle.

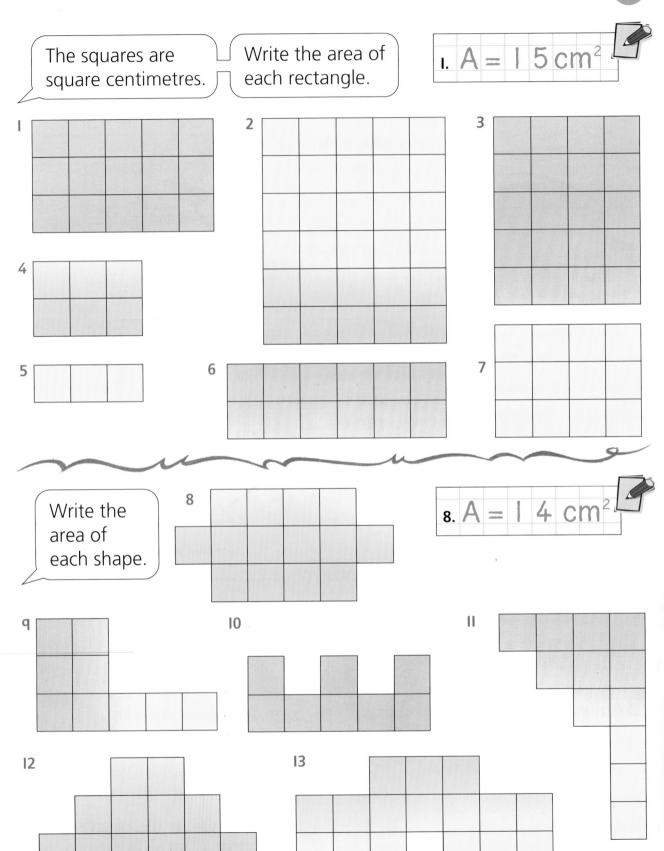

1. $A = 15\,\text{cm}^2$

Write the area of each shape.

8. $A = 14\,\text{cm}^2$

Area

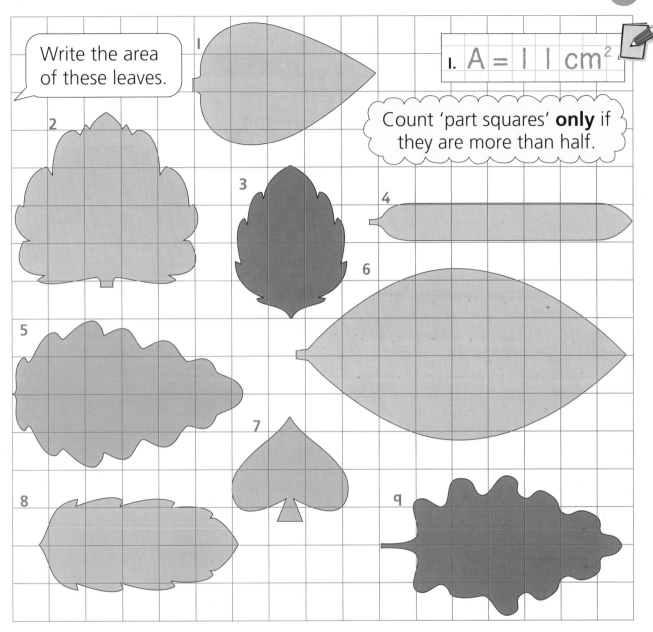

Write the area of these leaves.

1. $A = 11\text{ cm}^2$

Count 'part squares' **only** if they are more than half.

Explore

Draw 10 different rectangles on squared paper.

Cut them out.

Put them in order (smallest to largest area) by estimating.

Find each area. Write the area on the rectangles.

Was your estimated order correct?

The squares are square centimetres. Write the area of each shape.

1. $A = 9\,cm^2$

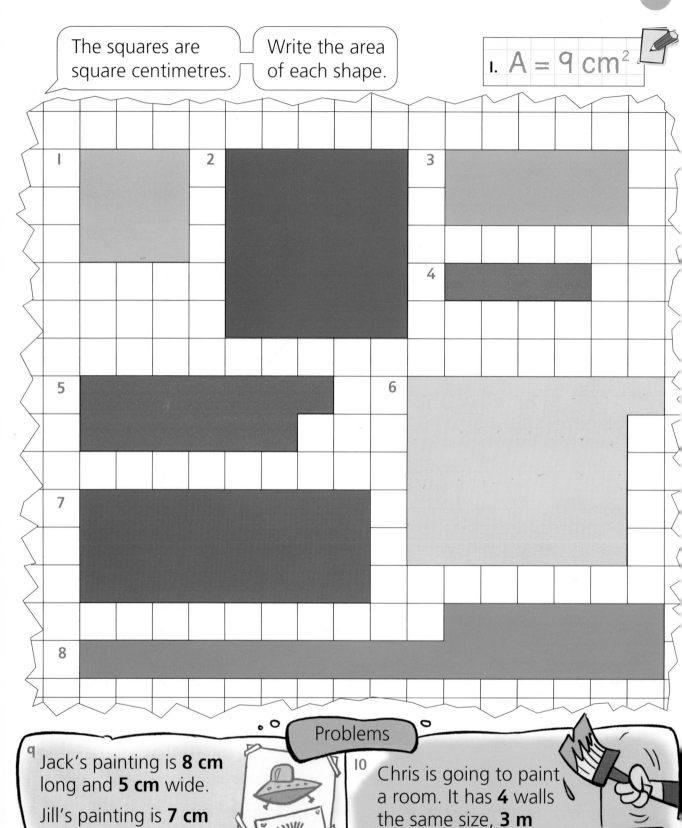

Problems

9. Jack's painting is **8 cm** long and **5 cm** wide.

Jill's painting is **7 cm** long and **6 cm** wide.

What is the difference in area?

10. Chris is going to paint a room. It has **4** walls the same size, **3 m** high and **8 m** long.

A tin of paint covers **32 m²**. How many tins will he need?

Perimeter and area

> Write the perimeter of each shape.

I

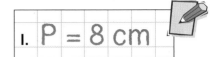
1. $P = 8$ cm

2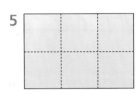

3

4

6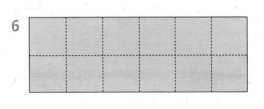

5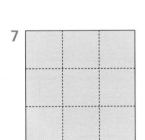

8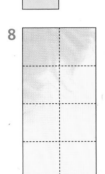

q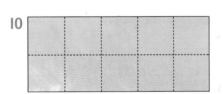

7

10

> Which 3 shapes have the same perimeter?

e Write the area of each shape.

Explore

Draw a square I cm by I cm on squared paper. Write its area and perimeter.

Draw a square 2 cm by 2 cm. Write its area and perimeter.

Continue drawing squares with sides I cm longer each time.

Write the area and perimeter each time.

What do you notice?

Can you guess the area and perimeter of the I0th square?

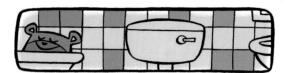
The tiles in Ted's bathroom are I cm square.

Write the perimeter and area of the blue shapes.

1. $P = 8$ cm
   $A = 3$ cm^2

℮ Write the total area of blue tiles.

This shape has a perimeter of I0 cm.

Draw other different shapes with a perimeter of I0 cm.

Use squared paper.

Perimeter

Each garden is rectangular.

Write the number of metres of fence needed to go round the edge.

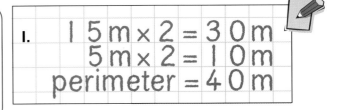

I.
$$15m \times 2 = 30m$$
$$5m \times 2 = 10m$$
$$perimeter = 40m$$

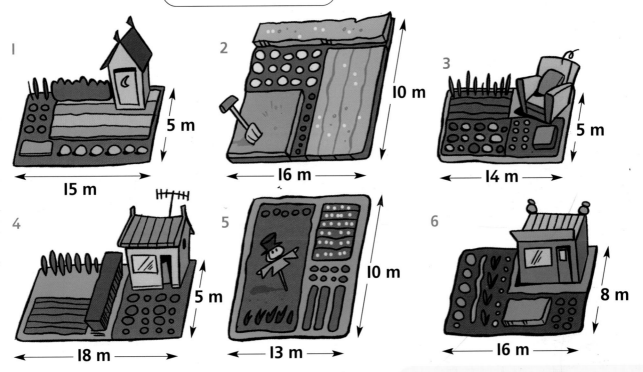

1   5 m   15 m

2   10 m   16 m

3   5 m   14 m

4   5 m   18 m

5   10 m   13 m

6   8 m   16 m

e Find the area of each garden.

Problems

7 George is decorating the cake.

The top cake is **20 cm** by **30 cm**.

The bottom cake is **40 cm** by **50 cm**.

He wants to put ribbon around each cake.

How much does he need?

8 Marka puts green tape round the edge of her notebook.

She uses **100 cm** of tape.

Suggest some possible measurements for the notebook.

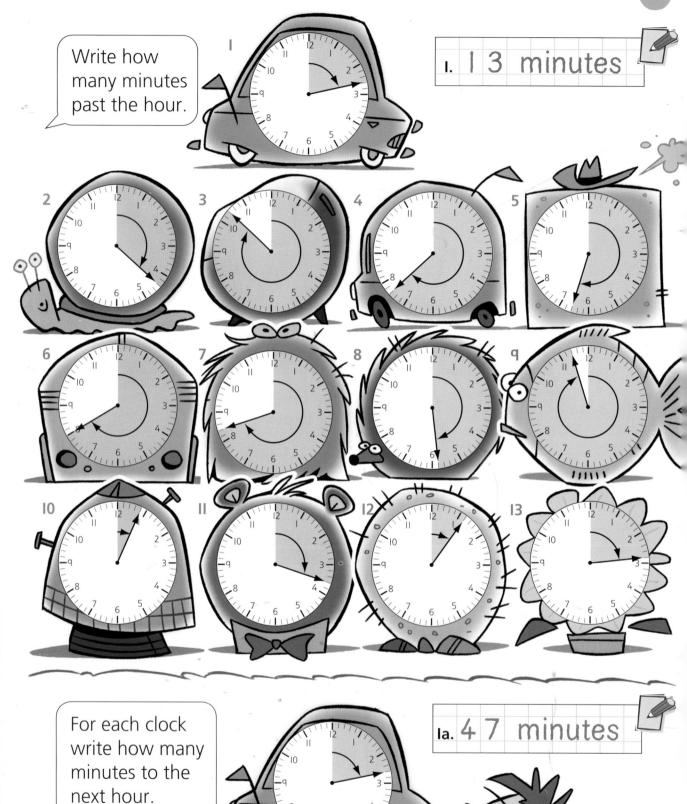

Write how many minutes past the hour.

1. | 3 minutes

For each clock write how many minutes to the next hour.

1a. 4 7 minutes

Telling the time

Write the times.

I. 20 past 9

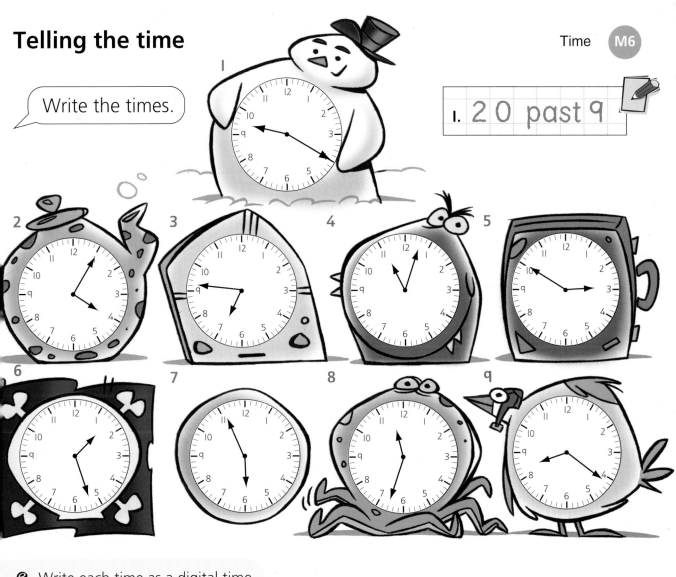

e Write each time as a digital time.

Write how many minutes between each pair of clocks.

?

Telling the time

Write the pairs of clocks that match.

1. l and f

ⅇ Write each time 11 minutes later.

Problems

8 Vijay's alarm goes off at **7:30 a.m.**

He gets up **10 minutes** later.

He takes **42 minutes** to get ready.

School is a **15 minute** walk away.

When does he get to school?

9 Jess sets the video for **9:10 p.m.**

The film is **90 minutes** long.

The film starts **5 minutes** late.

The video goes off at **10:50 p.m.**

Has it recorded Jess' film?

a.m. and p.m.

Time M6

Write each time.

Write a.m. or p.m. beside it.

1. 7:20 a.m.

2

3

4

5

6

7

Draw or write what you might be doing at each time.

8  11:30 AM

9  1:30 PM

10  10:15 AM

11  2:12 AM

12  7:30 AM

13  7:30 PM

14  12:10 PM

15  5:50 AM

21

November

Sun	Mon	Tue	Wed	Thu	Fri	Sat
	1	2	3 Ill, day off school	4	5	6 Bonfire party
7 Simmi's party	8	9 Go swimming	10	11 Museum trip	12	13
14	15	16	17	18	19 Cinema	20 Football match
21 Wildlife park	22	23 Dentist	24	25	26	27 Christmas shopping
28 Visit Gran	29	30				

Write the dates.

1 Bonfire party   **1.** 6 November

2 Football match   3 Dentist   4 Cinema

Write the days.

5 Wildlife park   **5.** Sunday

6 Go swimming   7 Museum trip   8 Ill, day off school

How many days after the Museum trip is the:

9 Cinema

10 Dentist

11 Christmas shopping

Calendars

January						
Su	M	Tu	W	Th	F	Sa
	1	2	3	4	5
6	7	8	9	10	11	12
13	14	15	16	17	18	19
20	21	22	23	24	25	26
27	28	29	30	31		

February						
Su	M	Tu	W	Th	F	Sa
					1	2
3	4	5	6	7	8	9
10	11	12	13	14	15	16
7	18	19	20	21	22	23
24	25	26	27	28		

March						
Su	M	Tu	W	Th	F	Sa
					1	2
3	4	5	6	7	8	9
10	11	12	13	14	15	16
17	18	19	20	21	22	23
24	25	26	27	28	29	30
31						

April						
Su	M	Tu	W	Th	F	Sa
	1	2	3	4	5	6
7	8	9	10	11	12	13
14	15	16	17	18	19	20
21	22	23	24	25	26	27
28	29	30				

May						
Su	M	Tu	W	Th	F	Sa
			1	2	3	4
5	6	7	8	9	10	11
12	13	14	15	16	17	18
19	20	21	22	23	24	25
26	27	28	29	30	31	

June						
Su	M	Tu	W	Th	F	Sa
						1
2	3	4	5	6	7	8
9	10	11	12	13	14	15
16	17	18	19	20	21	22
23	24	25	26	27	28	29
30						

Write how many:

1 Wednesdays in January   1. 5

2 Tuesdays in February   3 Fridays in April

4 Mondays in March   5 Sundays in June

What day is the first of:

6 January   6. Tuesday

7 April   8 June   9 May   10 March

What is the last day of:

11 February   12 June   13 May

14 January   15 April   16 March

Write the number of weekend days in each month.

17. January → 8

Calendars

Write the months of the year in order.

January

July

February

December

August

May

April

November

June

September

October

March

Write the number of days in each month.

J M M J A S O N D
F A J J S N

1. January 3 1 days

1	January	2	March	3	October
4	June	5	April	6	August
7	July	8	May	9	September
10	November	11	February	12	December

Saturday	Channel 8
9:00	Rab and Rob
9:20	Bonzo the Dog
9:50	Strange Hill School
10:15	Dragon Quest
10:30	Animal Watch
11:30	Space Cops
12:30	Brainiac Quiz
1:00	News
1:10	Weather

Write the start times.

1   Animal Watch   1. 10:30

2   News   3   Space Cops   4   Brainiac Quiz

5   Rab and Rob   6   Dragon Quest   7   Strange Hill School

Write the end time for each.   1a. 11:30

Which programmes start at these times?   8. Space Cops

8   9   10   11

❷ Write the length of each programme.

Timetables

Josh and Meg have planned their Saturday.

Our Saturday	
8:30	Breakfast
8:50	Dress and wash
9:10	Watch TV
9:45	Play in garden
10:05	Go to the park
12:00	Lunchtime
12:30	Wash up
12:55	Tidy rooms and change
1:30	Go to Jo's
2:00-5:30	Jo's party

How much time do they spend:

I   at breakfast?   I. 20 minutes

2   in the garden?

3   at Jo's party?

4   having lunch?

How much time between starting:

5   breakfast and finishing lunch?

6   to tidy their rooms and going to Jo's?

7   to play in the garden and the end of Jo's party?

8   to watch TV and going to the park?

9   lunch and finishing the washing up?

Write your own timetable for next Saturday.

My Saturday
8:30 Get up

Timetables

How long does it take from the bus station to:

Blue Zone 133		
 Bus station	7:40
YUM YUM'S Supermarket	7:45
School	8:50
Town hall	8:56
Post office	9:02
Library	9:14
Hospital	9:17
Train station	9:22
Swimming pool	9:42
Bus station	9:50

1     I. 5 minutes

2   3  4

How long does it take from:

5  to

6  to

7 to    8  to   9 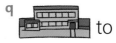 to

10  to   11 to    12  to

℮ The bus does the whole route again at 3:30. Write the times for each stop.

Explore

Find the length of time between each stop on the timetable.

Write them in order.

Which is longest/shortest?

Seconds

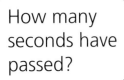

How many seconds have passed?

l. 2 0 seconds

For each clock above, write how many seconds to the next minute.

la. 4 0 seconds

Seconds

> Write how many minutes and seconds.

I. **I minute I5 seconds**

1	75 seconds	2	92 seconds	3	110 seconds
4	96 seconds	5	130 seconds	6	125 seconds
7	91 seconds	8	122 seconds	9	84 seconds

Runner	Raj	Bec	Ben	Jill	Mani	Marcos	Jess	Fi	Tim
Time (seconds)	79	160	86	182	94	95	84	88	152

> Which children finished in:

10 under $1\frac{1}{2}$ minutes?

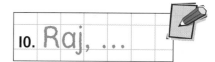

10. **Raj, ...**

11 between $1\frac{1}{2}$ and 2 minutes? 12 between 2 and $2\frac{1}{2}$ minutes?

13 between $2\frac{1}{2}$ and 3 minutes? 14 over 3 minutes?

> Who finished:

15  first?

16  third?

17  fifth?

✐ Write the children's names in the order they finished.

Seconds

> Write how many seconds.

1. 1 minute 20 seconds

ı. 8 0 seconds

2. 1 minute 5 seconds
3. 1 minute 40 seconds
4. 1 minute 7 seconds

5. 1 minute 52 seconds
6. 2 minutes 12 seconds
7. 2 minutes 10 seconds

8. 1 minute 35 seconds
9. 2 minutes 20 seconds
10. 2 minutes 40 seconds

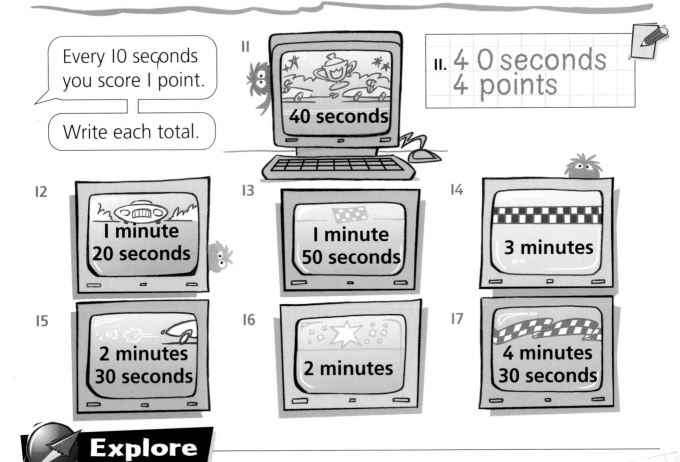

> Every 10 seconds you score 1 point.

> Write each total.

11. 40 seconds

ıı. 4 0 seconds
4 points

12. 1 minute 20 seconds

13. 1 minute 50 seconds

14. 3 minutes

15. 2 minutes 30 seconds

16. 2 minutes

17. 4 minutes 30 seconds

Explore

Use a calculator.

Find how many seconds in:

(5 minutes) (half an hour) (an hour)

Find how many seconds in other lengths of time.

Seconds

Write the time you estimate is closest.

1. 150 seconds

2 | 150 | 500 seconds

2

5 | 55 | 200 seconds

3

10 | 30 | 200 seconds

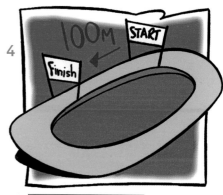

4

30 | 200 | 1500 seconds

5

10 | 240 | 2000 seconds

6

10 | 60 | 100 seconds

7

10 | 60 | 1000 seconds

Problems

8 Each game is timed.

Each game lasts between **30** and **60 seconds**.

What is the largest number of games possible in **10 minutes**?

Find the fewest games possible.

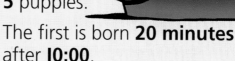

9 Sheba has **5 puppies**.

The first is born **20 minutes** after **10:00**.

The rest are all born **600 seconds** apart.

What time is the last puppy born?

Polygons

Are these polygons?

Write 'yes' or 'no'.

I. yes

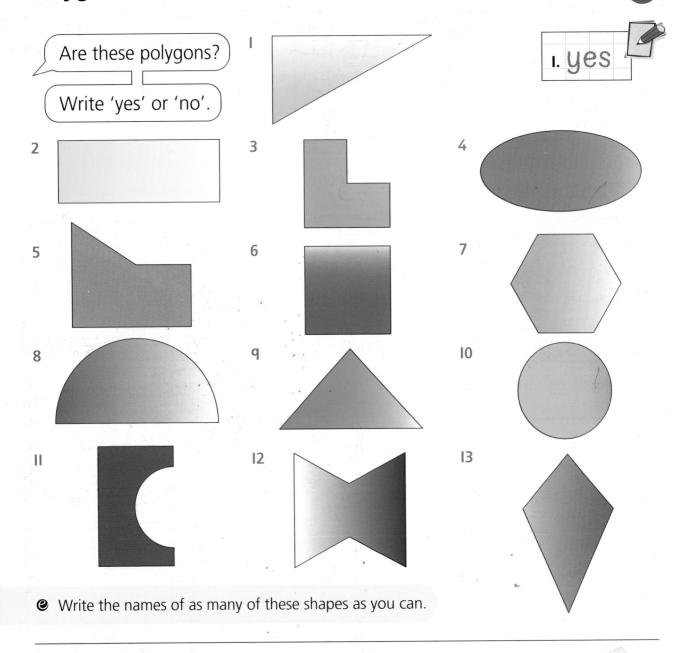

❷ Write the names of as many of these shapes as you can.

Draw 6 shapes of your own.

3 polygons
3 not polygons

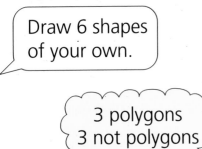

polygons

triangle ⫶ quadrilateral ⫶ pentagon ⫶ hexagon ⫶ heptagon ⫶ octagon

Write the name of each polygon and the number of sides.

1. octagon, 8

Draw these polygons:

15 quadrilateral   16 heptagon

17 triangle   18 octagon   19 hexagon

14 pentagon

14.

Naming polygons

Write the name of each polygon and the shape of each hole.

1. pentagon, rectangle

1

2

3
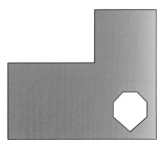

4

5
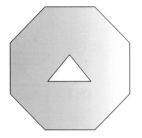

6

7
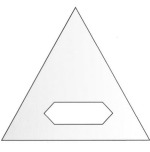

8

9
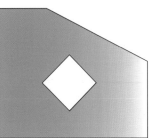

Draw these:

10 a pentagon with a triangular hole

10.
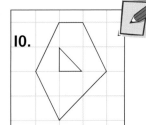

11 a quadrilateral with a pentagonal hole

12 an octagon with a rectangular hole

13 a pentagon with a hexagonal hole

14 a triangle with a circular hole

Regular polygons

Are the polygons regular?

Write 'yes' or 'no'.

1

I. yes

2

3

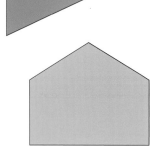

4

5

6

7

8

9

10

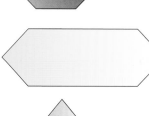

11

12

13

Write the name of each polygon.

I. regular hexagon

Explore

Draw a set of different irregular polygons.

Draw polygons with 3, 4, 5, 6, 7 and 8 sides.

Label each one.

Isosceles and equilateral triangles

Name each triangle.

Write 'isosceles' or 'equilateral'.

1. equilateral

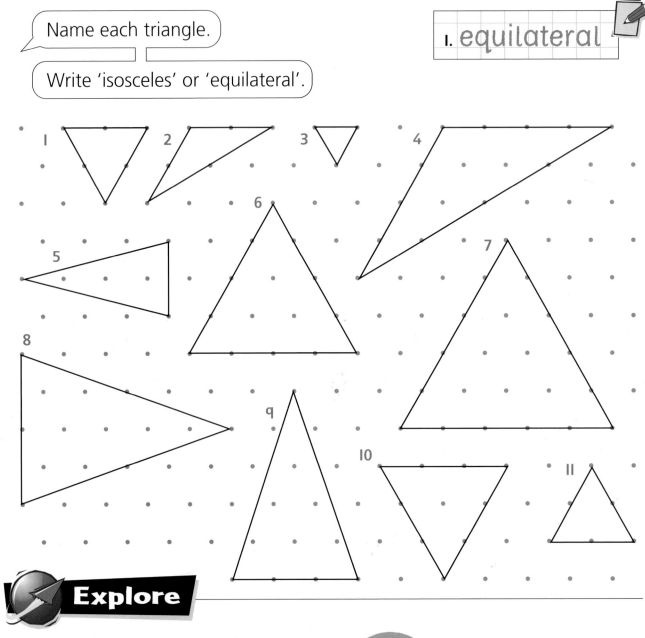

Explore

Make an equilateral triangle.

1 Draw round a large circular shape.

2 Mark the centre.

3 Fold from any part, into the centre.

4 From one end of your first fold, fold into the centre again.

5 Fold the last part to make an equilateral triangle.

Isosceles triangles

Are these isosceles triangles? — Write 'yes' or 'no'.

1. no

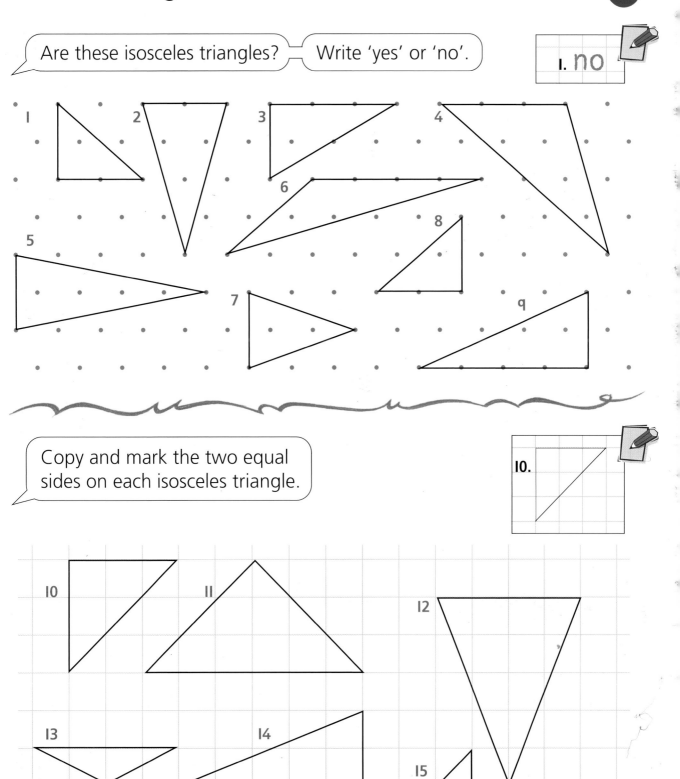

Copy and mark the two equal sides on each isosceles triangle.

10.

Symmetry

Are these lines of symmetry? — Write 'yes' or 'no'.

Use a mirror to help you.

1. yes

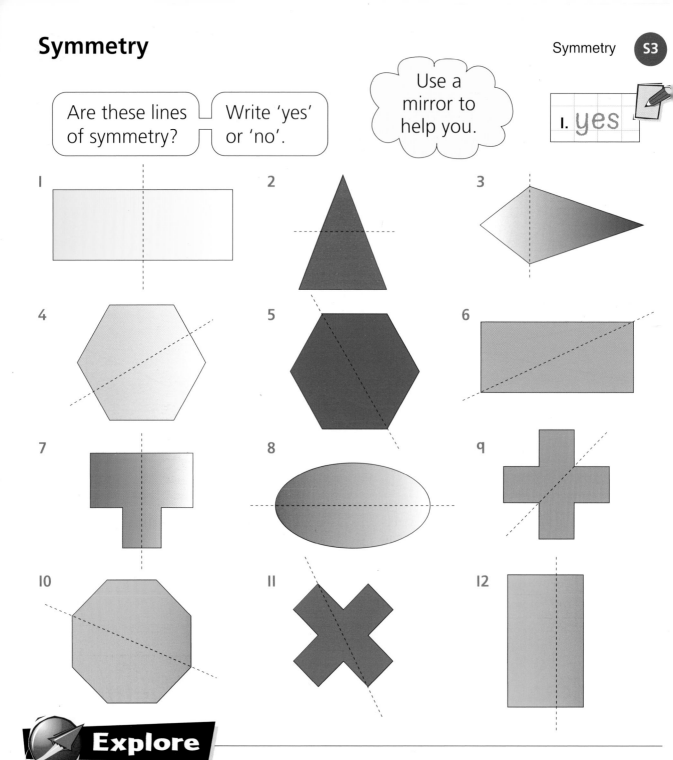

1 **2** **3**

4 **5** **6**

7 **8** **9**

10 **11** **12**

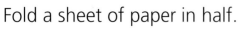

Explore

Fold a sheet of paper in half.

Draw a shape along the fold.

Cut it out, then open the paper.

Count the sides.

Can you make a 4-sided, 5-sided, ... shape?

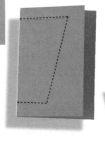

Symmetry

Copy on squared paper.   Draw each shape's reflection.

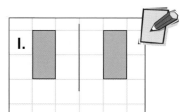

I.

1
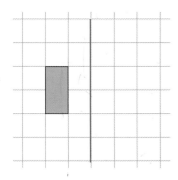

2
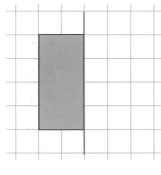

3
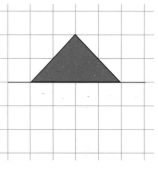

4
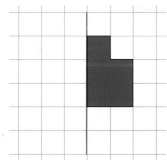

5
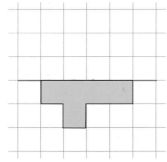

6
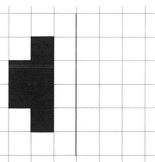

7
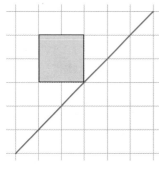

8
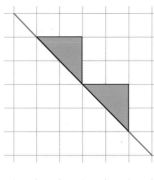

9
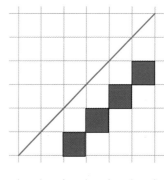

10
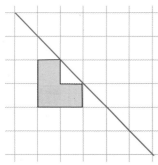

11
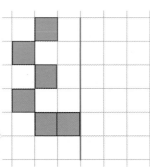

12
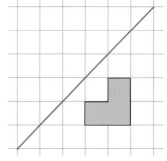

Draw 3 more symmetrical pictures.   Use squared paper.   Draw the line of symmetry first.

Symmetrical patterns

Copy on squared paper. | Complete to make a symmetrical pattern.

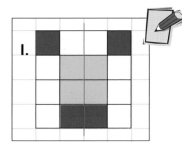

1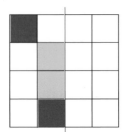

2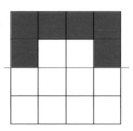

3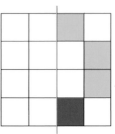

4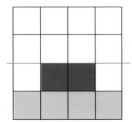

5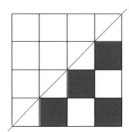

6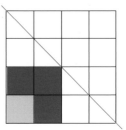

7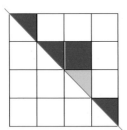

8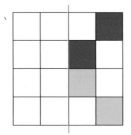

q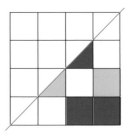

Draw three 6 by 6 grids.

Draw 2 lines of symmetry on each.

Draw three symmetrical patterns with a line symmetry of 2.

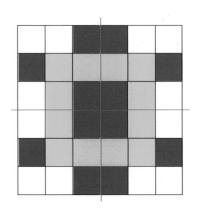

40

Nets

Are these shapes the nets of cubes? Write 'yes' or 'no'.

1. yes

1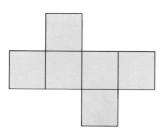

2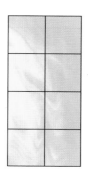

3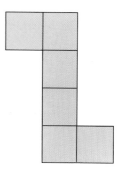

4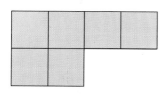

5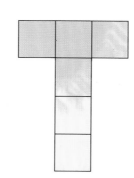

6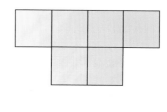

7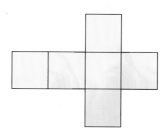

8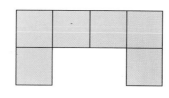

q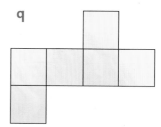

Use the net of a cube. Draw spots on the faces. Fold it and stick it to make a dice.

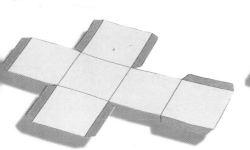

Nets

cube   cuboid   pyramid   prism

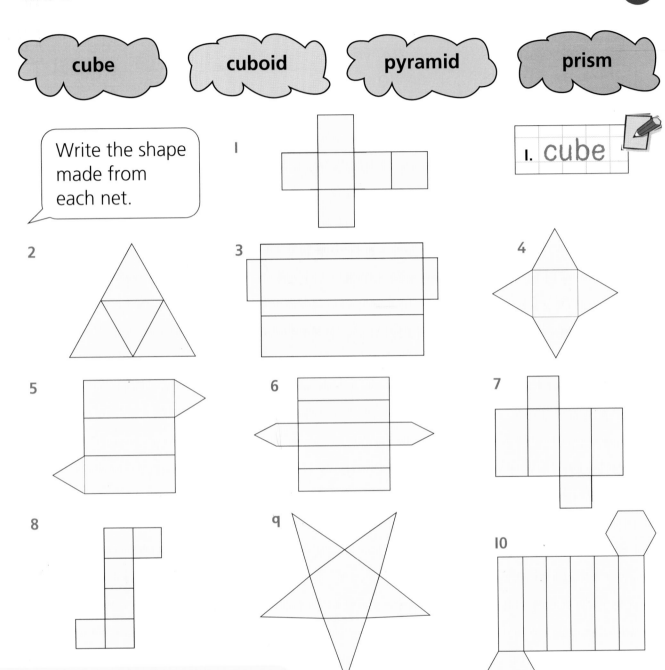

Write the shape made from each net.

1.

I. cube

2

3

4

5

6

7

8

q

10

☺ Choose a net and make the shape.

For each shape, write the number of:

I. a. 6   b. 8   c. I 2

a faces   b vertices   c edges

Prisms and pyramids

3-d shape **S4**

Name each shape. Write 'pyramid' or 'prism'.

1. triangular prism

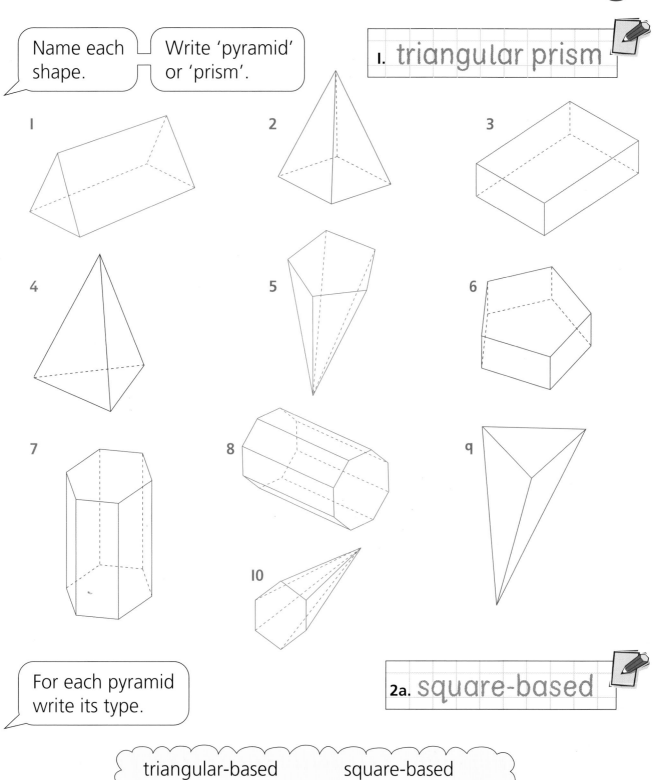

1

2

3

4

5

6

7

8

9

10

For each pyramid write its type.

2a. square-based

triangular-based   square-based
pentagonal-based   hexagonal-based

𝒆 Which of the pyramids are tetrahedrons?

43

Compass points

> Write the direction each bird is facing.

1. east

2

3

4

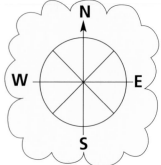

5

6

7

8

9

10

11

12

> Write the direction each bird faces after one half turn.

1a

1a. west

 Explore

North and south are **opposite** directions.

Write the other pairs of opposite directions.

44

Compass points

Direction S5

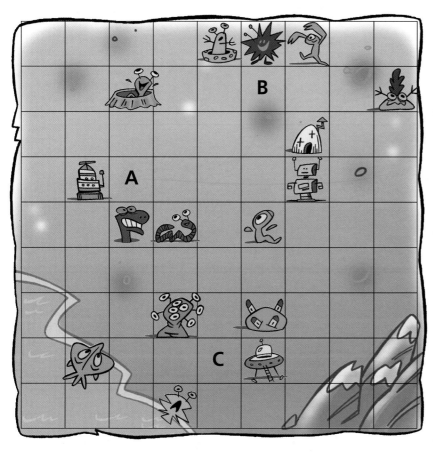

Alien Adventure

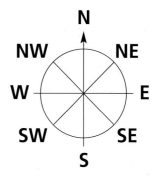

From A, what direction is:

 2
 3

1

I. south

 8
 9

From B, what direction is:

4
5

6
7

From C, what direction is:

 14
 15

8
9

10
11

12
13

16
17

45

Compass points

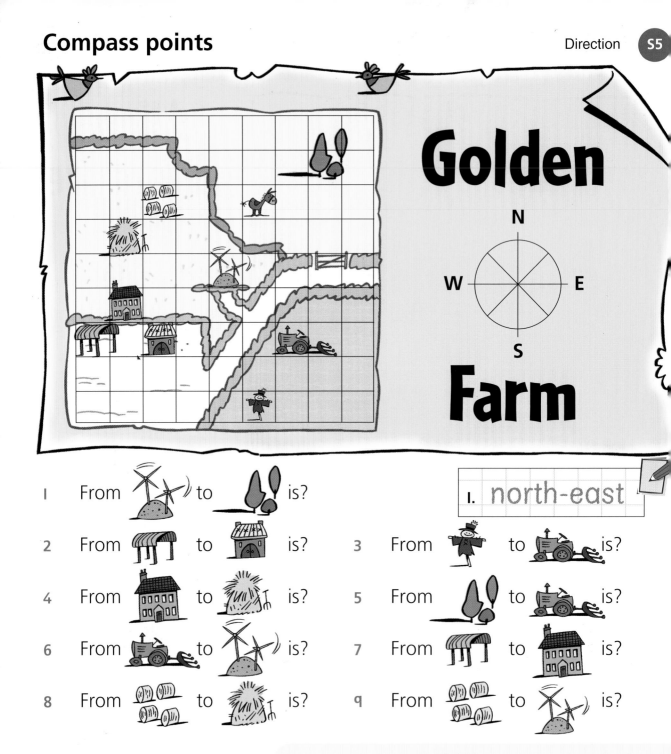

Golden

N
W   E
S

Farm

1   From 🪁 to 🌳 is?

                        I. north-east

2   From 🛖 to 🏠 is?   3   From 💂 to 🚜 is?

4   From 🏠 to 🌾 is?   5   From 🌳 to 🚜 is?

6   From 🚜 to 🌀 is?   7   From 🛖 to 🏠 is?

8   From ⬤ to 🌾 is?   9   From ⬤ to 🌀 is?

e Write the direction of different objects from the horse.

Explore

Use a road atlas.

Write a place **north** of your school.

Find places in other directions.

Turning

Write the direction of the train before and after each turn.

1

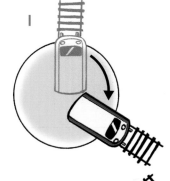

1. north to south-east

N

NW   NE

W   E

SW   SE

S

2

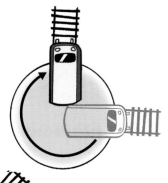

3

4

5

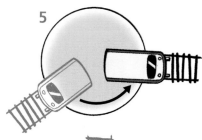

6

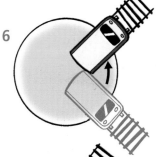

7

8

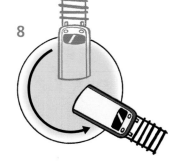

9

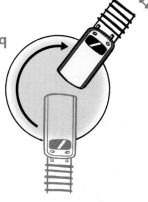

Write how many right angles for each turn above.

1a

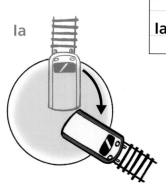

1a. $1\frac{1}{2}$ right angles

Angles

Write the direction before and after each turn.

I. **north to south**

1

180°

2

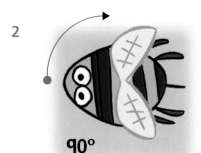

90°

3

180°

4

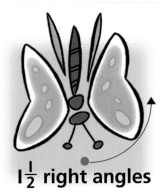

$1\frac{1}{2}$ **right angles**

5

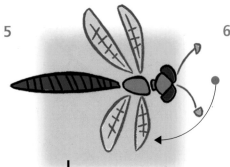

$2\frac{1}{2}$ **right angles**

6

45°

7

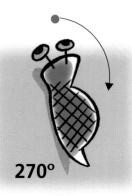

270°

8

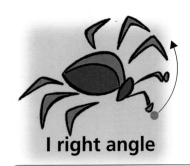

I right angle

9

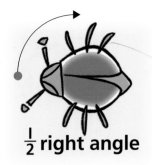

$\frac{1}{2}$ **right angle**

10

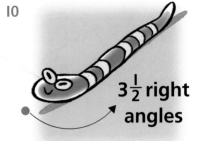

$3\frac{1}{2}$ **right angles**

Write 'clockwise' or 'anticlockwise' for each turn above.

Ia. **clockwise**

Explore

Write 4 different turns that finish facing south-east.

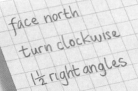

face north
turn clockwise
$1\frac{1}{2}$ right angles

Angles

The **minute** hand turns by the angle shown. Write the new time.

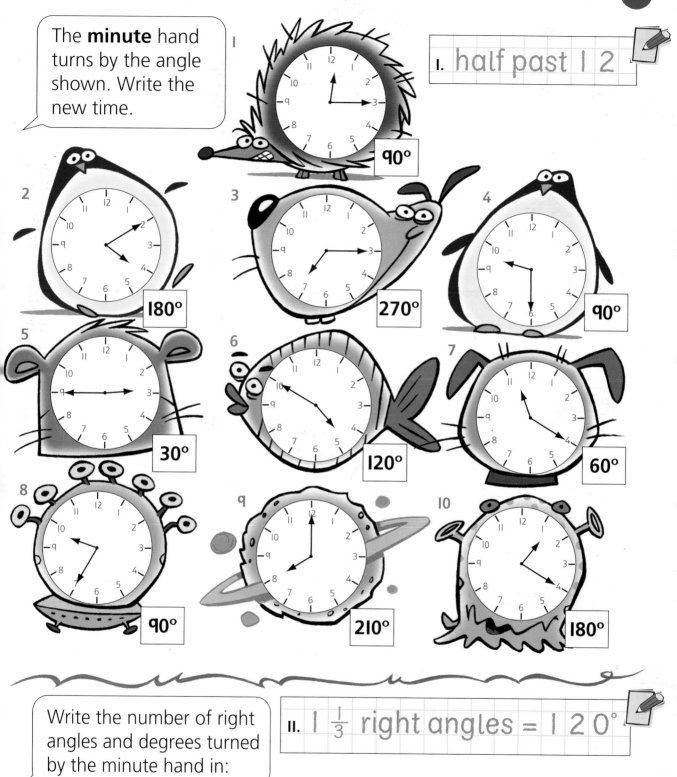

1. 90°

I. half past 12

2. 180°

3. 270°

4. 90°

5. 30°

6. 120°

7. 60°

8. 90°

9. 210°

10. 180°

Write the number of right angles and degrees turned by the minute hand in:

II. 1 ⅓ right angles = 120°

11	20 minutes	12	5 minutes	13	30 minutes	14	45 minutes
15	10 minutes	16	35 minutes	17	15 minutes	18	50 minutes

Coordinates

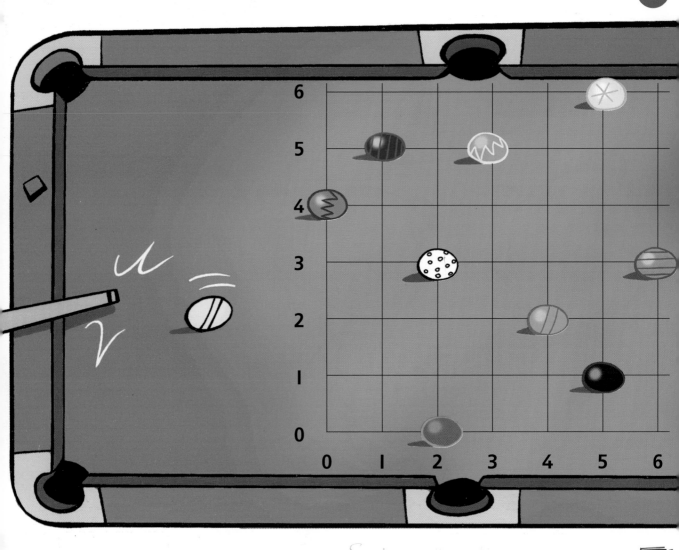

Write how far each ball is **along**.

 1

 1. 5

2   3   4   5

6   7   8   9

Write how far each ball is **up**.

la. 1

Write the coordinates of each ball.

lb. (5, 1)

Coordinates

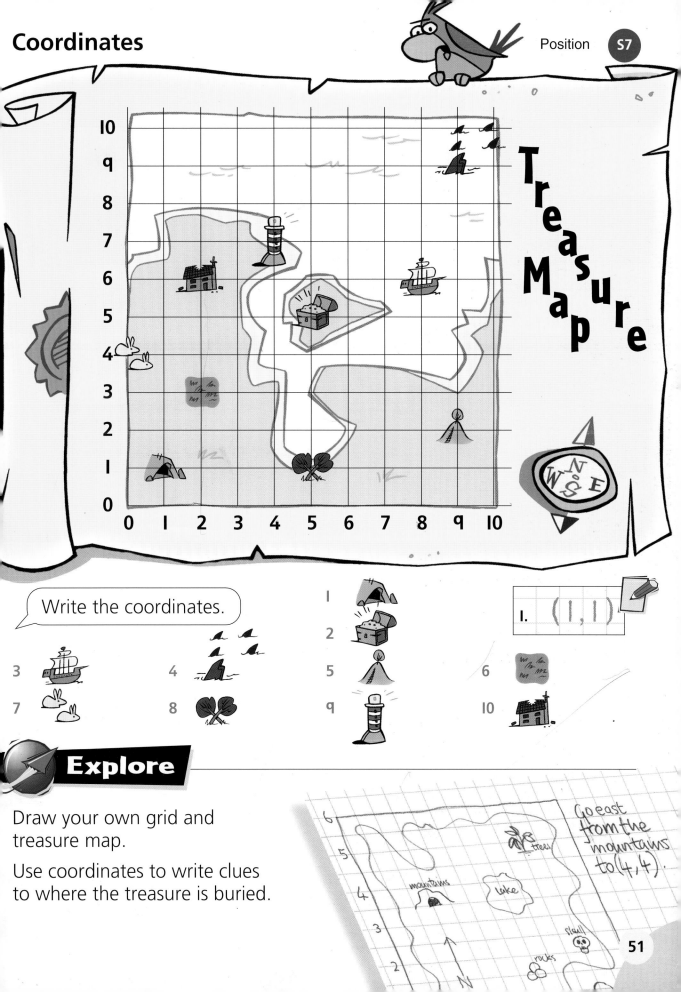

Write the coordinates.

1		2			1. (1, 1)
3		4		5	6
7		8		9	10

Explore

Draw your own grid and treasure map.

Use coordinates to write clues to where the treasure is buried.

Go east from the mountains to (4,4).

mountains   lake   trees   skull   rocks

51

Coordinates

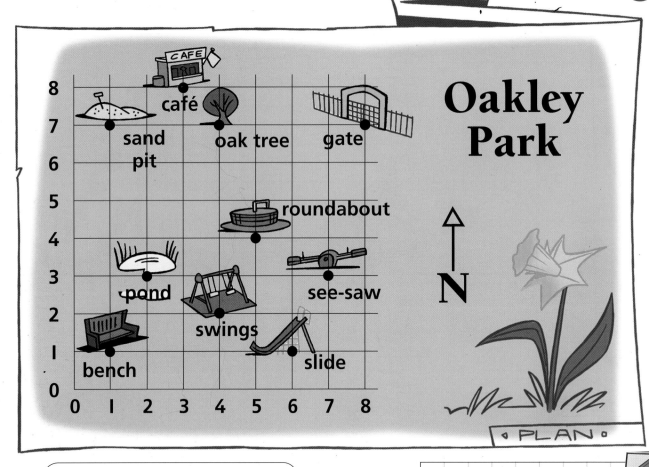

Oakley Park

PLAN

Write what is at each point.

I. roundabout

I	(5, 4)	2	(4, 7)	3	(1, 1)	4	(6, 1)	5	(7, 3)
6	(2, 3)	7	(8, 7)	8	(3, 8)	9	(1, 7)	10	(4, 2)

Problems

II Jon is on the swings.

He walks 2 squares north-east, then I square west.

Where is he now?

12 Bob is on the slide.

He walks 5 squares north-west and I square north.

Where is he now?

13 Ellen is on the see-saw.

She walks 4 squares north and 6 squares south-west.

Where is she now?

Frequency tables

aeiou

> Count how many times each vowel appears in the rhyme.

> Copy and complete the table.

Vowel	Frequency
a	
e	
i	
o	
u	

> As I was going up the stair
> I met a man who wasn't there.
> He wasn't there again today
> Oh how I wish he'd go away.

> Which vowel appeared:

| 1 | 7 times? | 2 | 6 times? |

1. i

3   12 times?   4   least?   5   most?   6   second most?

> Which of these appeared most often?

7. e, 1 more

7   e **or** i   8   e **or** u   9   i **or** o

10   o **or** u   11   a **or** e   12   u **or** a

Explore

Find a short piece of writing.

Count the frequency of each vowel.

Draw a frequency table and write about the results.

Frequency tables

Our favourite T.V. programmes

Programme	Total votes
The Odd family	32
Robodog	15
Clever Class	22
Animals, animals	45
Space Cops	10
Junior Street	20
Top Tunes	30

Write which programmes had these votes.

1 20

I. Junior Street

2 22   3 32

4 most   5 second most   6 fewest

Write how many voted for:

7 Space Cops   8 Top Tunes

9 Robodog   10 Animals, animals

11 Space Cops or Top Tunes   12 Clever Class or Robodog

Explore

25 children chose their favourite colour from red, green, blue and yellow.

Red had most votes.

Yellow had fewest votes, only 3.

Red had double green's votes.

Draw some different frequency tables to show the possible votes.

Frequency tables

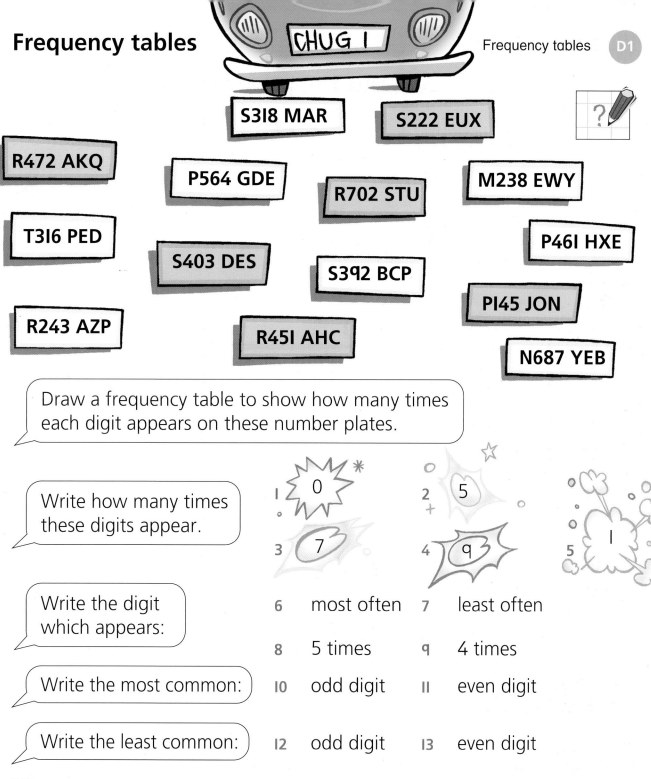

CHUG 1

S318 MAR   S222 EUX

R472 AKQ

P564 GDE

R702 STU

M238 EWY

T316 PED

S403 DES

S392 BCP

P461 HXE

PI45 JON

R243 AZP

R451 AHC

N687 YEB

Draw a frequency table to show how many times each digit appears on these number plates.

Write how many times these digits appear.

1 0   2 5
3 7   4 9   5 1

Write the digit which appears:

6 most often   7 least often

8 5 times   9 4 times

Write the most common: 10 odd digit   11 even digit

Write the least common: 12 odd digit   13 even digit

Explore

Collect 10 phone numbers.

Find the frequency of different digits.

Write about your results.

The Telephone Directory

01865 31

55

Pictographs

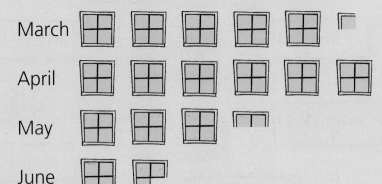

Days it rained, March to July

March

April

Months May

June

July

Number of days

Key

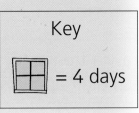
= 4 days

Write which month had:

1 most rainy days   2 fewest rainy days

Write the number of rainy days in:

3 June   4 March

5 May   6 July   7 March and April   8 June and July

Write how many more rainy days there were in:

9 April than June

10 May than July   11 March than May

Draw a pictograph to show the number of days it didn't rain in each month.

Pictographs

Goals scored this season

 Teams

Key	

=	
3 goals	

City

United

Rovers

Town

Rangers

 Number of goals

Write the teams that scored:

1   less than 15 goals   2   more than 15 goals

Write how many more goals these teams need to have 20.

3   City   4   Town

5   Rovers   6   United

Write the total goals scored by:

7   City and United   8   Rangers and Rovers   9   all teams

Explore

Write 5 questions for this pictograph.

Find the answers.

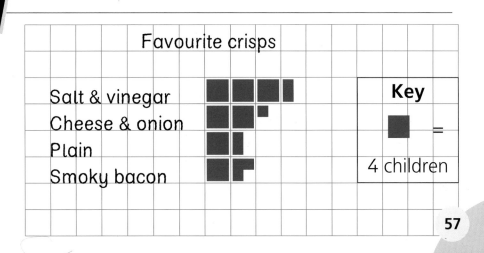

Pictographs

There were 75 sweets in a packet.

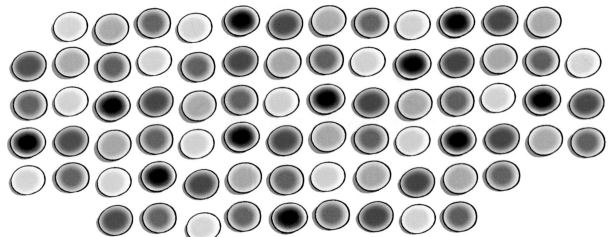

Draw a pictograph to show how many of each colour. | Use ⊕ to mean 4 sweets.

Write how many sweets are:

I	red	2	blue	3	yellow
4	black	5	pink		

Write the colours that had:

6   an odd number of sweets

7   an even number of sweets

Write how many sweets are:

8	red or pink	9	blue or yellow		
10	not black	11	not pink	12	not red

Write the colour which is:

13   most common   14   least common

Draw another pictograph to show how many of each colour, but ... | ... use this key. ⊘ = 3 sweets

58

Bar graphs

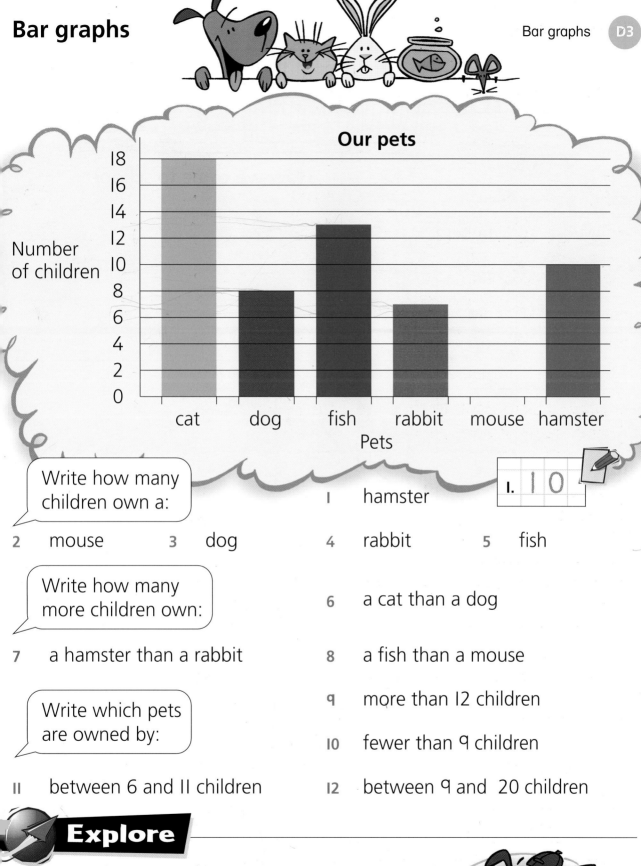

Our pets

Number of children

cat   dog   fish   rabbit   mouse   hamster

Pets

Write how many children own a:

1 hamster

1. | 1 | 0 |

2 mouse   3 dog   4 rabbit   5 fish

Write how many more children own:

6 a cat than a dog

7 a hamster than a rabbit   8 a fish than a mouse

9 more than 12 children

Write which pets are owned by:

10 fewer than 9 children

11 between 6 and 11 children   12 between 9 and 20 children

Explore

Ask 20 children what pet they would like to own
Draw a bar graph to show the results.

Bar graphs

How we come to school

Transport	Number of children
car	20
bike	7
foot	12
coach	5
bus	9
roller-blades	2
other	4

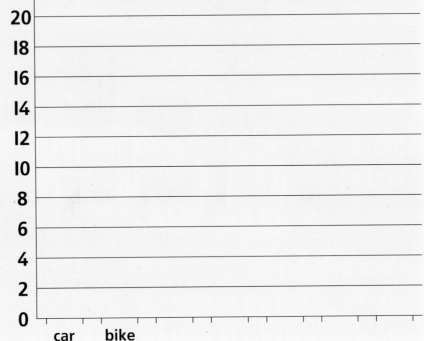

Copy and complete the bar graph.

Remember to label your graph and give it a title.

Write how many children come to school by:

I car **or** coach

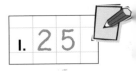

I. 2 5

2 bus **or** bike   3 foot **or** roller-blades   4 bus **or** coach

Write how many more come by:

5 foot **than** bike   6 car **than** coach

7 car **than** bus   8 bus **than** coach   9 car **than** bike

Bar graphs

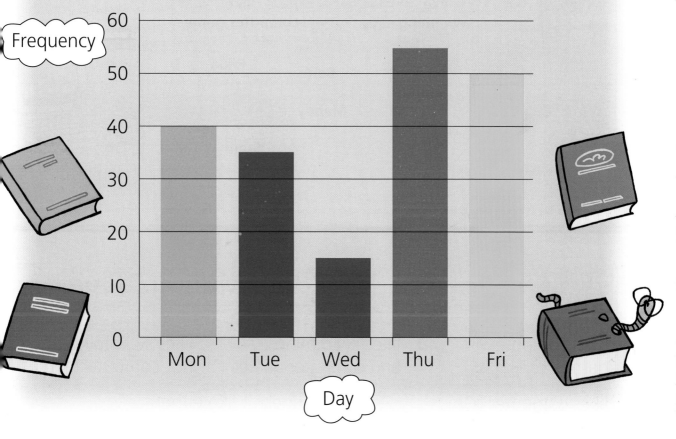

Library books borrowed last week

Frequency

Day

Write how many books were borrowed on:

I   Thursday   2   Monday

3   Friday   4   Wednesday

Write on which day:

5   most books were borrowed

6   fewest books were borrowed

Write how many books were borrowed:

7   on Monday **and** Tuesday

8   on Wednesday **and** Thursday   9   on the first 3 days of the week

10 on the last 3 days of the week   II in the whole week

Venn diagrams

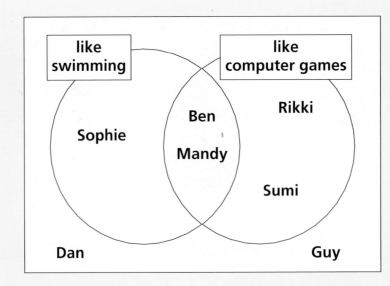

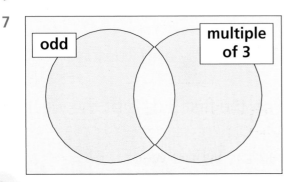

Write who:

1 likes swimming

1. Ben, Mandy, Sophie

2 likes computer games

3 likes swimming and computer games

4 likes swimming but not computer games

5 likes computer games but not swimming

6 doesn't like either

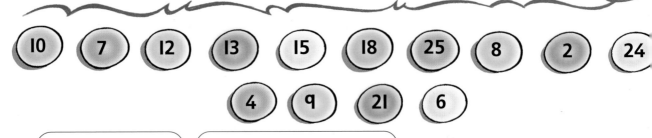

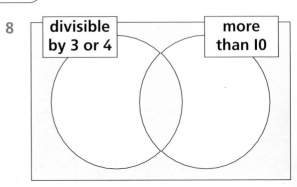

Copy each Venn diagram. Write the numbers in the correct position.

7

odd   multiple of 3

8

divisible by 3 or 4   more than 10

Carroll diagrams

	has a brother	has no brother
has a sister	Jon Suzie	Karen Sean Ruth
has no sister	Amit	Matt Beni

Write who has:

| a brother

I. Jon, Suzie, Amit

2 a sister

3 no brother

4 a sister but no brother

5 a brother but no sister

6 a sister and a brother

7 no brothers or sisters

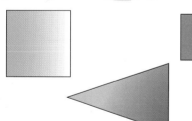   

Copy the Carroll diagrams. **Draw the shapes in the correct positions.**

8

	polygon	not a polygon
quadrilateral		
not a quadrilateral		

q

	regular polygon	not a regular polygon
triangle		
not a triangle		

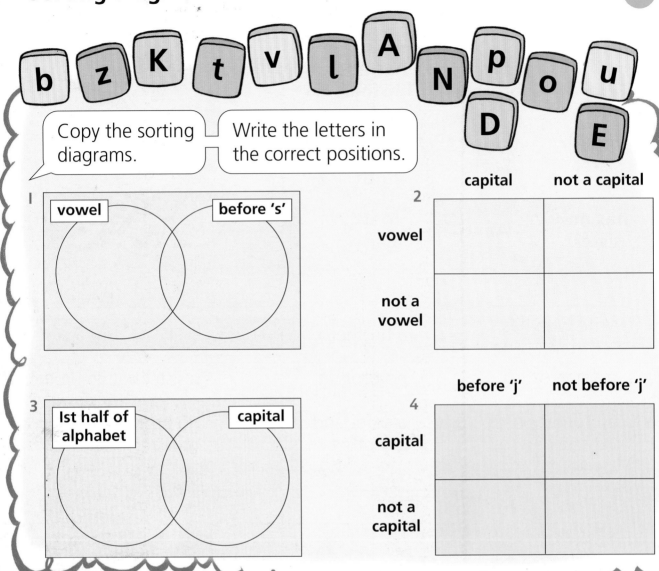

Copy the sorting diagrams.

Write the letters in the correct positions.

1. vowel — before 's'

2.

	capital	not a capital
vowel		
not a vowel		

3. 1st half of alphabet — capital

4.

	before 'j'	not before 'j'
capital		
not a capital		

Use number cards 1 to 10.

Make 4 labels: odd   even   multiple of 3   more than 5

Choose 2 labels.

Draw a Venn diagram and write the numbers in the correct positions.

Which numbers are in the overlap?

Repeat for different pairs of labels.

How many times does each number appear in the overlap?

Which numbers don't appear in the overlap? Why?